Affirmations for Wealth

250 Positive Affirmations About Living in Abundance Now and Attracting Money

Contents

Introduction

You are what you think, said Earl Nightingale in his famous book "The Strangest Secret". You become what you think about most of the times. If a person feeds his mind with negative thoughts, he will experience life through a dark lens. Small things that shouldn't affect him will become bigger than they really are as the mind is focused on the worst instead of the best. A person living with mostly negative thoughts has a mind focused on problems, instead of opportunities. Now, do you want to know a sad truth? Most people live in a such a mind. And can you really blame them? Most of the media outlets certainly do not help us to achieve a blissful state of mind. Their mantra is "negative news sells" and thus they engage in fear mongering. And do you want to know another sad truth? It works darn well for them. The reason it works is because we humans are designed to survive and not to thrive. While it is good for our species that our brain has its default mode focused on survival, it doesn't guarantee personal success. If it did, we'd see more people flourishing both personally and financially.

Now the good thing for you is that you're already ahead of most people as you certainly are aware of the power of the mind. You probably already know that your mind is like a strong computer capable of incredibly impressive things. Your job is like that of a programmer's. You need to stay guard at the doors of your mind and feed it with empowering words.

This book can help you if you want to live in a state of abundance. Furthermore, by using the affirmations within this book, you'll hopefully be able to spot opportunities for creating wealth that you were unable to see before. To benefit the most from this book, it's recommended you pause and reuse an affirmation that you feel particularly resonates with you. Also, for affirmations to work effectively, you must put your heart into the ideas being presented. Leave the sceptic at the door and trust the process so you can reach your goals and dreams! Let's begin, shall we?

A Few Words About Using Affirmations Effectively

Firstly, state the affirmation in the present tense. Your goal is to feel as if you already have the things you want, no matter the outer circumstances. This will help you attract what you want in the present.

Secondly, your affirmations must only contain positive words. The reason to avoid negative words such as 'no', 'never' or 'not' is that your subconscious cannot process negative words. Instead, it removes the negative words so for example an affirmation stating, "I'm not poor" will become I'm poor" which is the opposite of what you want.

Thirdly, affirmations should be specific and deal with one goal at the time. You can have several affirmations about different topics but aim to keep the individual affirmation focused.

Fourthly, it's recommended to practice an affirmation at least 20 times thrice a day. Continue this practice until your mind completely accepts the affirmation as true. Once it does, repeat the affirmation on a continuous basis to reinforce the effect of that suggestion. Strive to make the daily use of affirmations a lifelong practice.

Keep these important ideas in mind and adhere to them when creating a personal affirmation. This will ensure you affirm the right suggestions and set you up for success.

Chapter 1 – 50 Gratitude Affirmations

"When you are grateful, fear disappears and abundance appears."
- Tony Robbins

Gratitude is the foundation for living in a state of abundance and without it, you won't find true fulfilment as your mind never appreciates the abundance you already have. Think about it, you live better than a king did just a couple of centuries ago. One could argue that you even life better than a king did only a couple of decades ago since you have such useful technology at your disposal. I among many other people also believe that gratitude will attract more good things into one's life, including wealth. So, when you go through these affirmations, aim to feel gratitude and express them as if you're the wealthiest person in the world. Speak them with confidence and use your body in a way that will create emotion. Remember that motion creates emotion so by using your body in a confident way, you'll benefit the most from these affirmations.

1. I am grateful for living in the 21st century.

2. I am so thankful for all the money that I have.

3. I feel appreciation for the things money allows me to buy.

4. I love life and I'm so grateful to be a part of it.

5. I know that life is a gift.

6. While I inhale, I take full pleasure of the air that energizes my body and mind.

7. I am so grateful for the opportunities life has given me.

8. I'm so grateful for the opportunities life is continuing to give me.

9. I feel gratitude towards people for I know that they can help me achieve my dreams.

10. I am so grateful for who I am since I know that I can create magnificent things.

11. I am grateful for being in control.

12. I feel grateful for the people in my life.

13. I am grateful for the opportunities to come.

14. I was given the gift of life and the chance to make whatever I want of it, and for that I am grateful.

15. I am grateful for all the resources that I have and those that are to come.

16. I am grateful for my resourcefulness and my ability to find solutions.

17. I see the good in events and people.

18. I know that the chances of me being born were very low and I am so grateful for beating the odds.

19. Gratitude is my antidote to fear and anger. I am now in control of my emotions.

20. I am so grateful for my ability to produce.

21. Every day, I am living life to the fullest as a thanks to God for giving me the gift of life.

22. I am so grateful for my prosperous future.

23. I am grateful for my health, wealth, love and happiness.

24. An abundance of money is flowing to me right now and for that I am grateful.

25. I am so grateful that people treat me with respect and care for my well-being.

26. I am so grateful for having all my needs meet.

27. I give thanks to the Universe for allowing me to live my dreams.

28. I am the master of my life and for that, I am grateful.

29. I am so grateful for being able to use the wonderful things that others have created.

30. I am grateful for all the money ideas that come to me.

31. I know that one only needs to be right one time to become financially prosperous and I am grateful that it's my turn now.

32. I am grateful for I know that successful people want to help me, be it via books, videos or in person.

33. I am grateful for the abundance of choices I've been given.

34. I know that freedom is uncertain for some people in other parts of the world, that's why I appreciate that I've been born here.

35. I am grateful for money.

36. I am free to live life on my own terms, and for that I am grateful.

37. I am grateful for the plenty of opportunities to create an abundance of money.

38. I know that my mind can create incredible things and for that, I am grateful.

39. I am so grateful for having multiple sources of income.

40. I am so grateful that money comes to me in avalanches of abundance from unexpected sources on a continuous basis.

41. I love all the events money can allow me to experience.

42. I am grateful for my incredible ability to solve problems and bring immense value to the market place.

43. I am grateful for my commitment to live in abundance.

44. I know that I can feel the feeling of abundance whenever I want, and for that I am so grateful.

45. I hereby give thanks to the Universe for all the prosperity I experience.

46. Money flows effortlessly to me and for that, I am grateful.

47. Gratitude is a gift of life and I experience it daily.

48. Abundance is a natural state for me and I love it.

49. I live better than hundreds of kings before me and for that, I am grateful.

50. I am so grateful that money flows with ease into my bank account.

Chapter 2 – 50 Abundance Affirmations

"When you focus on being a blessing, God makes sure that you are always blessed in abundance."
- Joel Osteen

To live a life of true abundance, we first must make a conscious decision to live in a beautiful state no matter what. Life does not happen to us, it happens for us and with that knowledge in mind, we can trust that the Universe is taking care of us and guiding us to the person we want to be as well as our desired place. So trust the process and choose to relax by breathing deeply whenever challenges arise. They are put in place to make you who God has intended you to be.

1. Gods wealth is circulating in my life.

2. I hereby chose to live in a beautiful state.

3. The Universe has my best interest at heart.

4. I experience avalanches of abundance and all my needs are met instantaneously.

5. Abundance is something we tune in to.

6. I choose to live in abundance in every moment of everyday for the rest of my life.

7. I know that I am being guided to my true self.

8. I live in financial abundance.

9. I know that my needs are always met and that answers are given to me.

10. Everyday in every way, I am becoming more and more abundant.

11. The Universe takes good care of me as I always have what I need.

12. My life is full of all the material things I need.

13. My life is filled with joy and love.

14. Money flows to me in abundance.

15. I have everything in abundance.

16. Prosperity overflows in my life.

17. My thoughts are always about prosperity and abundance.

18. My actions lead to prosperity and abundance.

19. I hereby focus on prosperity and abundance and thereby attract it into my life.

20. Abundance and prosperity is within me as well as around me.

21. I hereby allow all great things to come into my life.

22. I enjoy the good things that flows into my life.

23. I create prosperity easily and effortlessly.

24. I feel passionate about prosperity and thus it comes to me naturally.

25. I love abundance and I naturally attract it.

26. The whole Universe is conspiring to make me abundant and prosperous.

27. I let go of any resistance to abundance and prosperity and it comes to me naturally.

28. I am grateful for the prosperity and abundance in my life.

29. I am open and receptive to all the prosperity life is now willing to give me.

30. I am surrounded by prosperity.

31. I deserve to be wealthy.

32. My visions are becoming a reality.

33. Thank you Universe for all that you've given me.

34. I am a money magnet.

35. Prosperity is naturally drawn to me.

36. I am always using abundance thinking.

37. I am worthy of becoming financially prosperous.

38. I am one with the energy of abundance.

39. I use money to better my life as well as the lives of others.

40. I am the master of money

41. Money is my servant.

42. I can handle large sums of money.

43. I enjoy having an abundance of money.

44. I am at peace with large sums of money flowing to me.

45. Money leads to opportunities and experiences.

46. An abundance of money creates positive impact in my life.

47. It's my birthright to live in a state of abundance.

48. The Universe is guiding me to more prosperity right now.

49. Money is coming to me in large quantities and I am ready for it.

50. People want me to live in abundance and I know I deserve it.

Chapter 3 – 50 Affirmations about Attracting Money

"Thoughts become things. If you see it in your mind, you will hold it in your hand."

— Bob Proctor, You Were Born Rich

Money tends to come to those who have a prosperity mindset. The gratitude and abundance affirmations that we've gone through in previous chapters should have lifted up your invisible money magnet so you can start attracting an abundance of wealth into your life. The following are 50 affirmations about attracting money.

1. I'm filled with joy and gratitude and I love that more and more money is flowing to me continuously.

2. Money is flowing to me in avalanches of abundance from unexpected sources.

3. Money is coming to me faster and faster.

4. I deserve prosperity and to have an abundance of money in my bank account.

5. All my dreams, goals and desires are met instantaneously.

6. The Universe is on my side and it is guiding me towards wealth.

7. The Universe is guiding wealth towards me.

8. I love money and all that it can buy.

9. I feel grateful that I increase my net worth substantially every year.

10. Money flows to me with ease.

11. Ideas to make more money is coming to me often.

12. I feel good about money.

13. I can do good things with money.

14. I am worthy of prosperity and having an abundance of money.

15. I release all my negative beliefs about money and allow for financial abundance to enter.

16. Money is always close to me.

17. Opportunities to make more money come to me effortlessly.

18. I give value and money loves me for it.

19. I attract money with ease and I now have more wealth than I ever dreamed possible.

20. I am wealthy, and I feel incredibly good about it.

21. I have a great relationship with money.

22. I am gracious for all the money that I have.

23. Every day and in every way, I am attracting more money into my life.

24. Being wealthy feels fantastic.

25. I attract money effortlessly.

26. I now allow for money to flow freely into my life.

27. I am a money magnet and money will always be attracted to me.

28. I am now relaxing into greater prosperity.

29. I release all opposition to money.

30. I deserve to have a lot of money in my bank account.

31. Ideas of making money is freely entering my life.

32. Abundance is all around me and I feel so gracious about it.

33. Being wealthy is my natural state.

34. The Universe is helping me to attract money into my life right now.

35. I am prosperous, and I appreciate all the good things in my life.

36. I am affluent.

37. It feels phenomenal to have a lot of money in my bank account.

38. I love money and money loves me.

39. It's very easy for me to make more money.

40. I am a natural born money maker.

41. I am willing and ready to receive more money now.

42. My income increases substantially each year.

43. I happily receive money with ease.

44. The Universe keeps giving me more and more money.

45. Attracting money is easy for me.

46. Money is good and with it I can help other people better their life.

47. Financial success is my birth right.

48. An avalanche of money is transporting itself to me.

49. I feel good about receiving large quantities of money.

50. Thank you Universe for allowing me to live in prosperity.

Chapter 4 – 100 Success and Wealth Affirmations

"Your positive action combined with positive thinking results in success"

- Shiv Khera

In this chapter, we'll go through affirmations you can use to get a successful mind. What is a successful mind? Well it's a mind that contains positive and empowering beliefs about success regarding all aspects of life. It has been said that people fear success more than failure, and with that mindset, it is hard to achieve anything extraordinary. The affirmations below will not only help you overcome any subconscious blocks that might be holding you back from living your dreams, but they will also prime your mind to spot any wealth creating opportunities and more importantly; encourage you to act on them.

1. My beliefs shape my reality.

2. I realize that I'm the creator of my life.

3. I decide to make my life a masterpiece.

4. I know that if I believe it I can see it.

5. I have always been destined to become wealthy.

6. I find a lot of opportunities for creating prosperity and abundance.

7. I give and receive.

8. I live by the words "let go and grow". That's why I find it easy to forgive myself and others.

9. I'm grateful for the lessons my past has given me.

10. I'm a great giver; I'm also a great receiver.

11. I understand that my abundance of money can make the world a better place.

12. The universe responds to my mindset of abundance by giving me more prosperity.

13. I define my dream and feel gratitude for its realization.

14. I visualize living my dream every day.

15. I send out good vibrations about money.

16. I'm abundant in every way.

17. I'm grateful for all the money that I have. I'm grateful for all the prosperity that I receive.

18. I'm grateful for the present moment and focus on the beauty of life.

19. I pay myself first and make my money multiply.

20. I have a millionaire mind and I now understand the principles behind wealth.

21. I love the freedom that money gives me.

22. I'm a multi-millionaire.

23. I choose to be me and free.

24. There is an infinite amount of opportunities for creating wealth in the world.

25. I see opportunities for creating wealth and act on them.

26. My motto is act and adapt.

27. The answers always seem to come to me.

28. I have an attitude of gratitude.

29. I deserve to become wealthy.

30. I deserve to have the best in life.

31. I'm a wonderful person with patience.

32. I trust the universe to guide me to my true calling in life. Knowing this I get a feeling of calmness.

33. I know that I'm becoming the best I can possibly be.

34. I feel connected to prosperity.

35. I love money and realize all the great things it can do.

36. I'm at one with a tremendous amount of money.

37. Money loves me and therefore it will keep flowing to me.

38. I use my income wisely and always have a big surplus of money at the end of the month.

39. I truly love the feeling of being wealthy. I enjoy the freedom it gives me.

40. It is easy for me to understand how money works.

41. I choose to think in ways that support me in my happiness and success.

42. I'm an exceptional manager of money.

43. I realize that success in anything leaves clues.

44. I follow the formula of people who have created a fortune.

45. I create a lot value for others.

46. I'm a valuable person.

47. My life is full of abundance.

48. I know about the 80 20 rule which states that 80 % of the effects come from 20 % of the causes.

49. 20 % of my activities produce 80 % of the results.

50. I choose to focus on the most important things in my life.

51. I choose to become wealthy.

52. I make my money multiply by investing them wisely.

53. I pay myself first. 10 % of my income works for me.

54. Money works for me.

55. I increase my ability to earn by setting concrete goals and work to achieve them.

56. By implementing the 80 20 rule in my life I increase my productivity and profitability.

57. I focus on the most important areas in my life and eliminate, delegate or automate the rest.

58. Time is on my side now.

59. Everyday I'm getting better, smarter and more skillful.

60. I believe that other people want me to be successful and are happily helping me towards my dream.

61. I know how to handle people.

62. I smile often and remember the other person's name.

63. I give sincere appreciation and focus on the other person.

64. I make people feel important.

65. I praise improvement and call attention to people's mistakes indirectly. I make fault seem easy to correct.

66. I'm a great leader and people are happy about doing what I suggest.

67. I'm a good listener who encourages the other person to talk about him or herself.

68. I try honestly to see things from the other persons view.

69. I cooperate with others; whose minds work in perfect harmony for the attainment of a common definite objective.

70. I have a purpose and a plan.

71. I'm courageous and understand that courage is not the absence of fear but rather the willingness to act in spite of it.

72. I have self discipline and full control over my thoughts and emotion.

73. I do the most important things first.

74. I'm organized and remember the 80 20 rule.

75. I expect the best in life. I know about the magic of thinking big.

76. I always expect to win.

77. I'm a confident person who takes action.

78. I'm decisive and know what I want.

79. I'm committed to my success.

80. I know that where attention goes energy flows.

81. I see opportunities and act on them.

82. I write down my goals and program my subconscious mind for success.

83. I will persist until I succeed.

84. I only pray for guidance and I realize that I'm going to be tested.

85. I get stronger by challenges.

86. I live everyday as if it was my last.

87. I realize that life is a gift.

88. I'm grateful for being alive.

89. I understand that being born is a miracle and I'm very grateful for it.

90. I'm more than I seem to be and all the powers of the universe are within me.

91. I feel abundance and love.

92. I trust myself; my gut feeling knows the truth.

93. I harness my intuition and know that people might be like me, but that I'm unique.

94. My DNA and the way my brain is configured is completely unique.

95. I love myself and understand that I'm the only one who can be me.

96. I focus on my inclinations and the things I'm good at.

97. I develop my talents and abilities.

98. I focus on adding value.

99. The world will be a better place because I was here.

100. I'm a valuable person who takes responsibility.

Conclusion

My goal with this book was to leave you feeling empowered. I hope the affirmations herein has equipped you with the right mindset to attract more wealth into your life.

Remember what Tony Robbins said: *when you are grateful, fear disappears and abundance appears.* There's always something to feel grateful for no matter what so don't limit your gratefulness to only big events. Feel gratitude towards the air your breathing, the food you've got access to or the water you're drinking. Gratitude is the key to inviting more great things into your life and ultimately living a life of abundance.

Lastly, I would invite you to consider the power of habits. What I want said with this is that you can leave this book now and never return to it, and you will have benefitted from it. But if you come back to this book on a regular basis, you will integrate the changes on a much deeper level and that will lead to a more positive outcome in the long run.

I wish you all the best and I sincerely hope you'll enjoy life to the fullest!

Printed in Great Britain
by Amazon